I'M SORRY YOU CAN'T HATCH AN EGG
published by Gold 'n' Honey Books
a division of Multnomah Publishers, Inc.

© 1998 by Ray Butrum

Illustrations © 1998 by Jim Chapman

Design by Randy Robinson

International Standard Book Number: 1-57673-312-2

Printed in China

For information:
MULTNOMAH PUBLISHERS, INC.
POST OFFICE BOX 1720
SISTERS, OREGON 97759

98 99 00 01 02 03 04 — 10 9 8 7 6 5 4 3 2 1

I'm Sorry You Can't Hatch an Egg

By Ray Butrum
Illustrated by Jim Chapman

Gold 'n' Honey Books

I went to see my father's mom, who lives so far away.
I got to stay almost a month instead of just one day.

6

On my first day at Grandma's house I woke before sunrise.
I smelled good things cooking: bacon, biscuits, eggs, and pies.

"I'm glad you're up," my grandma said. "I need your help right now. Will you please go and fetch some eggs? Gramps will milk the cow."

I climbed up to the henhouse and the ladder gave a creak.
When I stepped in, to my surprise, a hen began to speak!
"Come here, young girl," the white hen clucked. "I know what you must do.
Go and look into my nest. There's something there for you."

14

"An egg!" I cried as I looked down at the golden nest of hay.
I reached and took the oval jewel, then turned to walk away.

"Be careful, dear," the chicken warned, "an egg takes time to make.
Although the shell may seem quite hard, if dropped, the egg will break.

"A broken egg's not helpful for either you or me.
It can't be cooked; it can't be hatched; it's just a waste, you see.
I'd like to make a chick with that, but I won't make a fuss.
You're having eggs for breakfast, so take it if you must."

"If I leave it here," I asked, "you can make a chick?
Show me how you do it—I'd like to learn this trick."

"It's not a trick," she said to me. "It takes too long to show.
But if I sat upon my egg, a chick would start to grow.

19

"For twenty-one days I'd keep it warm, and if everything went well,
In three weeks, the chick would hatch and live outside its shell."

"Then take it back," I said to her. "Here's what I will do—
I will sit upon an egg and hatch a chicken too!"

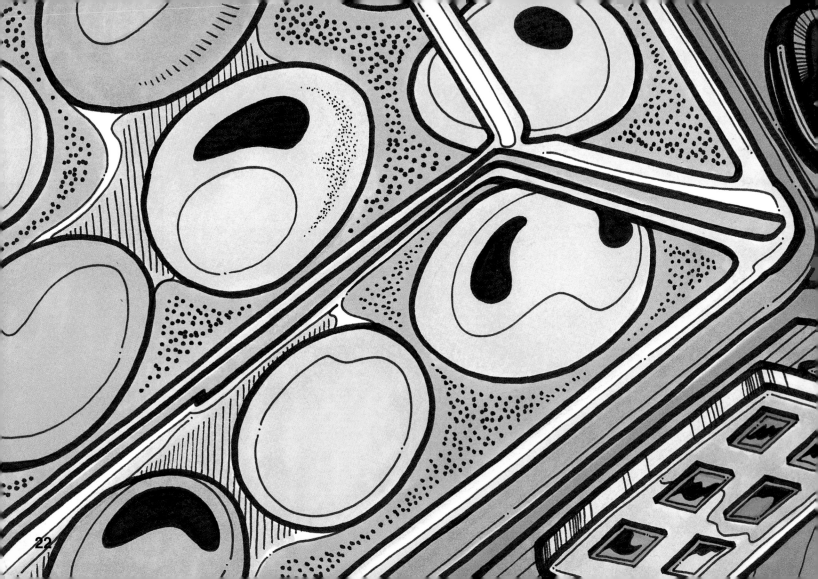

22

"I'm sorry you can't hatch an egg. But ask your grandma later
About the thing you'd have to use—it's called an incubator.
You see, I have these feathers that warm my egg just right.
The temperature must stay the same throughout the day and night."

The hen explained that life begins within the fragile shell.
A chicken's vital parts are formed from just one tiny cell.
"Tomorrow," said the friendly hen, "I'll save an egg for you
And do my best to hatch a chick before your visit's through.

24

25

"This will be our secret, just between us two.
Others might not understand that a hen has talked to you."

Then I left the henhouse and went back inside to eat,
Knowing that my visit here was going to be real neat.

27

CLUCK

Twenty-one days later, just as the hen had said,
A crack formed in the eggshell! Out popped a fuzzy head!
I always will remember the thing I learned that day:
Chicks aren't like human babies—they're born a different way.

Glossary

A **CELL** is the smallest unit of any living thing.

If something is **FRAGILE** it breaks easily.

To **HATCH** means to be born by breaking out of a shell.

An **INCUBATOR** is a container that keeps eggs warm.

A **NEST** is a bed of grass or straw an animal makes to protect its eggs or babies.

An **OVAL** is the shape of an egg.

A **SHELL** is the hard outer covering of a seed, an egg, or an animal.

At **SUNRISE** the sun comes into view over the horizon.